Money Smarts

Needs and Wants

by Nadia Higgins

Bullfrog Books

Ideas for Parents and Teachers

Bullfrog Books let children practice reading informational text at the earliest reading levels. Repetition, familiar words, and photo labels support early readers.

Before Reading

• Discuss the cover photo. What does it tell them?

• Look at the picture glossary together. Read and discuss the words.

Read the Book

• "Walk" through the book and look at the photos. Let the child ask questions. Point out the photo labels.

• Read the book to the child, or have him or her read independently.

After Reading

• Prompt the child to think more. Ask: Have you ever wanted to buy something? Did you need it? Or just want it?

Bullfrog Books are published by Jump!
5357 Penn Avenue South
Minneapolis, MN 55419
www.jumplibrary.com

Library of Congress Cataloging-in-Publication Data

Names: Higgins, Nadia, author.
Title: Needs and wants / by Nadia Higgins.
Description: Minneapolis, MN : Jump!, Inc., [2018]
Series: Money smarts
Includes bibliographical references and index.
Identifiers: LCCN 2017027411 (print)
LCCN 2017034479 (ebook)
ISBN 9781624966743 (ebook)
ISBN 9781620318928 (hardcover : alk. paper)
ISBN 9781620318935 (pbk.)
Subjects: LCSH: Basic needs—Juvenile literature.
Desire—Juvenile literature.
Classification: LCC HC79.B38 (ebook)
LCC HC79.B38 H54 2018 (print) | DDC 640—dc23
LC record available at https://lccn.loc.gov/2017027411

Editor: Jenna Trnka
Book Designer: Molly Ballanger
Photo Researcher: Molly Ballanger

Photo Credits: VaLiza/Shutterstock, cover (left), 6, 8; Ruth Black, cover (right); Gelpi/Shutterstock, 1; Kiselev Andrey Valerevich/Shutterstock, 3; wavebreakmedia/Shutterstock, 4, 5, 23bl; Erik Dreyer/Getty, 6–7, 8–9; Gareth Brown/Getty, 10; zulnazir/iStock, 11; wavebreakmedia/iStock, 12–13; Ovchinnikova Irina/Shutterstock, 14; Jose Luis Pelaez/Getty, 15; gorillaimages/Shutterstock, 16–17, 18–19; Jakub Krechowicz/Shutterstock, 18, 23tl; Tom Burlison/Shutterstock, 20–21 (foreground); Phonlamai Photo/Shutterstock, 20–21 (background); oksana2010/Shutterstock, 22tl; Nattika/Shutterstock, 22bl; Khajornkiat Limsagul/Shutterstock, 22tr; Darren Brode/Shutterstock, 22br; yingtustocker/Shutterstock, 23tr; Billion Photos/Shutterstock, 23br; kzww/Shutterstock, 24l; Mariyana M/Shutterstock, 24r.

Printed in the United States of America at Corporate Graphics in North Mankato, Minnesota.

Table of Contents

Needs Before Wants

It is lunchtime.

Bo wants dessert.

But what does
he need first?

Healthy foods.

Mic has money for a drink.

He wants soda.

Does he need it?

No.

His body needs water.

Mia and her mom shop.

Mia wants a pool toy.

But they need sunscreen.

First they buy sunscreen.

They have money left over.

Now Mia can buy a toy.

Tiff's dad gives her money at the store.

She needs fruit.

She wants fruit.

She buys apples.

Yum!

Zac wants
a snowboard.

But he needs
a winter coat.

14

His mom
buys him
a coat first.

bike

Rita wants a new bike.

Does she need it?

No.

Her bike works.

Rita saves her allowance.

Soon she will have
enough money.

She will buy
a new bike.

What do you need?

What do you want?

21

Need or Want?

What items are needs? What items are wants?

Picture Glossary

allowance
Money earned
for doing chores.

need
Something we need
to survive, such as
healthy food, water,
and shelter.

healthy
Good for
one's body.

want
Something we
would like but
don't need.

Index

To Learn More

Learning more is as easy as 1, 2, 3.

1) Go to www.factsurfer.com

2) Enter "needsandwants" into the search box.

3) Click the "Surf" button to see a list of websites.

With factsurfer.com, finding more information is just a click away.

THE★ UNITED STATES PRESIDENTS

CHESTER ARTHUR

Heidi M.D. Elston

Checkerboard
Library

An Imprint of Abdo Publishing
abdobooks.com

ABDOBOOKS.COM

Published by Abdo Publishing, a division of ABDO, PO Box 398166, Minneapolis, Minnesota 55439. Copyright © 2021 by Abdo Consulting Group, Inc. International copyrights reserved in all countries. No part of this book may be reproduced in any form without written permission from the publisher. Checkerboard Library™ is a trademark and logo of Abdo Publishing.

Design: Emily O'Malley, Kelly Doudna, Mighty Media, Inc.

Production: Mighty Media, Inc.

Editor: Liz Salzmann

Cover Photograph: Getty Images

Interior Photographs: Albert de Bruijn/IStockphoto, p. 37; AP Images, pp. 32, 36; David Caton/ Alamy, p. 33; Getty Images, pp. 20, 23, 31; Hulton Archive/Getty Images, p. 25; Library of Congress, pp. 6 (Edwin D. Morgan), 7 (Ulysses S. Grant), 10, 16, 17, 19, 21, 22, 24, 29, 40; National Archives, pp. 7 (Pendleton Act), 15, 27, 28; National Portrait Gallery/Smithsonian Institution, pp. 6, 14; North Wind Picture Archives, p. 13; Pete Souza/Flickr, p. 44; The Picture Art Collection/Alamy Stock Photo, p. 12; Shutterstock Images, pp. 7, 11, 38, 39; Stock Montage/Getty Images, p. 5; Wikimedia Commons, pp. 40 (George Washington), 42

Library of Congress Control Number: 2019956480

Publisher's Cataloging-in-Publication Data

Names: Elston, Heidi M.D., author.

Title: Chester Arthur / by Heidi M.D. Elston

Description: Minneapolis, Minnesota : Abdo Publishing, 2021 | Series: The United States presidents | Includes online resources and index.

Identifiers: ISBN 9781532193392 (lib. bdg.) | ISBN 9781098212032 (ebook)

Subjects: LCSH: Arthur, Chester Alan, 1829-1886--Juvenile literature. | Presidents--Biography--Juvenile literature. | Presidents--United States--History--Juvenile literature. | Legislators--United States--Biography--Juvenile literature. | Politics and government--Biography--Juvenile literature.

Classification: DDC 973.84092--dc23